Adventures
OF THE CLUMSY JUGGLER

Adventures of the Clumsy Juggler

OF THE Clumsy Juggler

Alan Gann

INK
BRUSH
PRESS

ISBN: 978-0-9888632-8-6
Library of Congress Control Number: 2014947779
Front Cover Painting: Marc Chagall, "The Juggler"
Photo on back cover: Neale Eckstein

Manufactured in the United States

Ink Brush Press
Dallas

Acknowledgments

My deepest thanks go to the Dallas Poets Community and the North Texas Songwriter's Collective; this book wouldn't have been possible without your insight and support. Special thanks to Michelle Hartman and Ann Howells whose cajoling and assistance went above and beyond the call of friendship.

I am grateful to the editors of the following journals for publishing some of the poems in this book.

Apratus Magazine
Cider Press
Dual Coast
First Literary Review–East
Fogged Clarity
Friend's Journal
Halfway Down the Stairs
Illya's Honey
In a Guilded Frame
Jack the Daw
KotaPress Poetry Journal
Luminosity
Main Street Rag
My First Time
nibble
North Texas Review
Plano Library Contest Anthology
Raleigh Review
Red River Review
Red Fez
San Perdro River Review

Sentence
Short, Fast, and Deadly
Sojourn
Texas Poetry Calendar
Visions and Voices
Yellow Mama
Zygote in My Coffee

Poetry from Ink Brush Press

For information on these and other Ink Brush Press books go to
www.inkbrushpress.com

CONTENTS

I. Practice

II. Busking

III. Taking a Bow

I. Practice

Tell me, what is it you plan to do
with your one wild and precious life?
—Mary Oliver

Four Pages From My Jesus Loves Me Coloring Book

On the Road to Bethlehem
I remember coloring Mary with child
blonde atop her brown donkey
because she looked like cousin Beth
riding her boyfriend's Harley.
Grandma said she didn't know
if Mary was a virgin,
but at least she'd gotten married
and to a carpenter who could support
a wife and kids.

Moneychangers in the Temple
Bet this is the only time I ever used
white crayons for anything but clouds—
having colored his face scarlet
he still didn't seem angry enough,
so I traced the steam
spewing from Yosemite Sam's ears.

One of You Will Betray Me
On thirteen empty plates
I used my new colored pencils
with their cone-sharpened points
to draw plump red wieners
on golden Wonder Bread buns
topped by thin streams of yellow mustard.

He is Risen!
Most meticulous page in the book—

Doubting Thomas fingering the wounds,
beautiful black beards, apricot skin,
shaded tan robes, red scars, yellow sun,
and then with metaphorical flourish
I added a full arcing rainbow.
If you look close, you can also find
six colored eggs hidden in the green grass.

The Story My Mother Told Me When I Fell Out of the Mulberry Tree

Some hobo carved
three lines suggesting a picnic table
into the whitewashed fence
separating my gandparents' house
from sparsely traveled Railroad Street
on the outskirts of Dixon Tennessee.

Having slipped out of the rattling boxcar
rail thin men, dusty beige to brown to black,
follow the crude map
and after pulling a drink from the well
sit quietly beneath the patient mulberry tree.

In a few minutes
the screen door clatters and Grandma serves
each a bowl of black-eyed peas and a biscuit.
She tries to make sure
every bowl has a tiny bit of fatback or bacon
and sometimes comes back
with a box of old shoes and shirts
collected from her Uncle's church.
Nobody speaks and the men keep their eyes
focused on the ground.

Through hand-sewn curtains
my mother watches these ghostlike men
until they disappear
then goes out and collects the dishes
scrubs them clean,

stacks them beside the cast iron stove
listening for the next distant whistle.

Juicy Questions

On our way home from Myrtle Beach
we always stopped
to buy firecrackers for the 4th
but sometimes older sisters get a wild hair
so one Sunday found myself
squirming in the backseat—
last hundred and twenty-five miles
with a pinch of itching powder down my shirt

like a real question tickles and I squirm
in the back row
until I can sneak away to the library
to the lab to the studio
scratch the yearning and discover for myself
why or how or what color the precipitate
(10 milliliters at the meniscus)
and maybe paint or dance or write
something the equations could not

the way Yahweh
looking out over the sixth dawn
pondering how to improve on perfection
squirmed until it was obvious
not even a god
should know with certainty
what will happen next

as I must pluck the golden apples
rhyme the unpronounceable name
turn the page
and squirming

peer through the lens
launch the bottle rockets
toss cherry bombs into the bonfire
and light all the sparklers at once.

14th Summer

and desire grows wild in creek-side brambles
free to pick take care the thorns
three in the pail one in the mouth
sticky sweet running down your chin

and first real kiss when my cousin sara
decided to lick the purple from these cheeks
we'd mount our bikes when first sun peaked
peddle to her special patch

and soon with buckets full and heavy
head home in time for breakfast
but first each checked the giggling other
for tick and scrape—careful combing

through sweaty hair and fingers running
long ticklish leg—lit match and tweezers
flash of teenage cotton,
neosporin and band-aids
that never completely staunched the flow

Second Base

The first time I got to second base
Kaylin called Sidney who told Sam
who posted a double-wow
on my facebook wall.

At breakfast,
Sara giggled when Mom set
two strategically placed strawberries
atop my pancakes,

and Dad asked
if I wanted to go to the farmer's market
and squeeze some melons.

Boy's Life: 1968 to 1977

from sunburn and pool bleached hair
secret blackberries passed down a chain of brothers
tom swift's deep sea diver and gilligan's island

from lawn mowers, johnny quest and spider bikes
shoe boxes with box turtles in 'em
backyard campouts and hair cut arguments

from dark shadows and streetlight basketball
scuppernong wine made in abandoned shacks
warm beer and playboys hidden in tree forts

from r-rated drive-ins and awkward explorations
talking her out of clothes
into things she'd already decided to do

Prayer for the South Valley
High Harvest Festival

God is good, God is twisted,
God is weird, confused, misunderstood—God is
every slump-shouldered who-cares hanging out by the
       skate park
boy who would rather write a story than shoot some
       hoops
girl who claims the boyfriend she's never had isn't
       missed
every band geek, orch dork, dweeb, and brainiac
computer nerd, stoner, bully, gamer, goth
door-slamming, eye-rolling, you-don't understand me
every funny fat kid, please-don't-call-on-me kid
timid artists with notebooks of sketched and shadowed
       dreams
each angry haircut, political t-shirt
extra ten pounds, ginormous zit
multitudes lost-in-the-shuffle B-averages
gawky, growing, golden globs of adolescence
willing to trade every milliliter of godliness
for one invitation to dance and courage to answer yes

Love Letters

Reflexively
alphabet begins with A
and simplest self-defining stroke
steps easily into both ideal and idiot,
but other words are less well built—
take dance—beige cousin against the wall
but dress it up in a flirtatious Q
graceful and cursive
on the arm of yearning partner
U as in jonquil
so when the band lifts their instruments
I will ask her to come and jonquil with me
across the floor out French doors
where full moon and billowing sky
like yellow and white blossoms
kiss
another word that just doesn't fit.
Sure esses sizzle but still too dry for passion
and the hard K unsmiling like a prison guard.
The onomatopoetic smooch
drips with possibilities but still
we need to wrap our tongues around
more syllables with an open ending
like Mallory with its fluttering Y
a rise of dragonflies
answering yes yes yes

Our Next Kiss

Our next kiss will be a jaguar crouched in a tree,
bull seeing red, and we will divide the dark
like a diver splits the surface,
lose our way as echoes in a too deep well.

Tonight's moon tumbles from her perch;
lizards vanish at the root. Slither through
the thicket with me and our next kiss
will be smoke on a burning river. Silent

as the library after midnight,
reliable as December's chill, I will come to you
and wrap your thighs in the fires of guilt.
Like the underside of a rotting trunk,

like a cat sleeping in the sun, our next kiss
will be opium from the pipe: slow as a heartbeat,
needy as a tomb—crawl toward the door,
rise and run deeper and deeper into the night.

The Manual Said

Stay calm. If capsized,
the SlimHull 250 will right itself,
so we neither feared nor fought the boiling rapids,
gave up futile attempts to steer our passage.

Like a fiberglass log,
we bounced boulder to boulder down The Devil's Chute.
Soaked and smiling; you looked back
and we toasted the ride with swigs of watery brew.

So this can hardly be a surprise.
Neon blue vest keeps my head above water,
gulping air, flailing arms.
Yellow helmet absorbs blows intended to crack and split.

My left leg might be broke
but these aquifers are chill and numb the pain.
So I cling to this low hanging branch
scan the surface for a glimpse of your red helmet.

Oh, and the canoe—last I saw
had righted itself, made it through the chute
headed merrily down the stream.

Windstorm

There's gonna be a tornado
when somewhere over the plains this humid wind
runs up against a cold air bank.

Perhaps she'll wander
harmlessly through an unplanted cornfield
or destroy a few houses just off Main Street. Maybe
she'll spare the trailer park, rip through the grasslands
or never touch down.
But there's gonna be a tornado tonight.

Once, when lightning struck a transformer,
left us candle lit,
Dad told stories about his year traveling with the
        carnival—
barking little towns from St. Paul to Abilene, described
every wall and funnel cloud—every hail storm and flood.

Later, on a blazing day, prisoner of the blue sky,
he asked, *Would you rather be a tornado or the sun?*
I am drawn to all that flame and heat,
but after 30 billion years of endless radiant days
even the most enthusiastic star might ask *God, is this all
        there is?*

Yes, there's gonna be a tornado tonight,
but it won't hit here.
All we'll get is sound and fury,
a light show and fallen branches.

The Making of a Clumsy Juggler

Three balls
blue, red and yellow
with a 6 page how-to pamphlet
stocking stuffer afterthought.

But gifts are fickle things
too cold to fly
the radio controlled biplane
so after dinner
I gave my first show
By half-time of the Cotton Bowl
a Beanie Baby turtle
added green to the spinning mix.

Stable of jokes
covered a multitude of fumbles
but nicknames
are also fickle gifts
and I wasn't given mine
until my junior year and tried
to date 3 cheerleaders on the same night

with girls
hidden in the closet
and slipping under the bed
like an episode of The Brady Bunch
and only poor Greg
doesn't know that the girls
figured it all out the day before.

My Semester in New York City

Mama didn't just up and die when she found out
I was sharing an efficiency
with a black lesbian named Djimbe Skyy.

Skipped Renaissance Ensemble to watch lightning
strikes over Central Park, barely caught the subway
in time for my Piano Composition class

Monet's *Water Lilies* Van Gogh's *Starry Night*

Joined a ska band called Crystal Night—
Quit after the ADL picketed our gig at the Bottom Line.

Thought I was the only person
from Farmville, North Carolina to eat a falafel sandwich
or have a friend named Qadeer.

At first we dressed in the bathroom,
but it was such a pain
and pretty soon I quit showing excitement if I saw…
well you know—didn't blush if she saw me.

It was a month
before I quit staring up at sky-scraped cityscapes.
Two months and I sneered at cricked-necked tourist.
After three, I just didn't give-a-shit.

But what I remember most is going home,
stepping off the bus—First thing my daddy says is
Come here boy, let me look at you.
Why you haven't changed a lick—not a lick.

Meditation on a Chrysanthemum

Molly sits lotus-legged in Chinese silk,
'til unseen tumblers finally click—

Let's eat; Let's dance; Let's screw 'til we're silly.
Molly lets me watch as she reassembles self,

walks with me toward our favorite little café,
but when I step fast to cross with the light

Molly turns left and is gone,
reappears when-wherever, beckoning hello,

tongues the labyrinth of my ear then bites the lobe.
As a drop of blood blossoms on cracked yellow tile,

she flips the switch and leaves me in the dark.

Blue and Wild

thunderless rain is just wet
but let the sky crack and sizzle
bellow groan and howl

on this turbulent night
anything that loves the world
must love me

and my dirty dishes
my unfinished novel
these sticky slices of golden mango

on this bottomless night
when my tongue lingers
around your too sweet belly

and every hair stands on end
rolling clouds flash rumble beat
discordant singing lusty and loud

for whatever loves this world
and feeds the untamed heather
everything that looks away or flies

yes on this fallen night yes
when your tongue does not linger
and the feral river churns

Venti Love

I will bring you Starbucks
certain as the vanishing night compels a reluctant dawn
corral dream-scattered synapses, refocus retinas,
ring coherence from erotic mutterings.

Or maybe
we'll forget steaming cups on the nightstand,
and for a few moments
shine brighter than any morning sun.
Then, while lattes cool,
sink back into that realm where mermaids sing
and sleep past noon.

Who Decides?

Orange juice is orange,
grape flavored Juicy Fruit is purple.
Lemon-yellow cough drops, strawberry lipstick red—
I get it, but who decided
my mint chocolate-chip ice cream should be
St. Patrick's Day shamrock, Three Mile Island meltdown,
acid hit neon, punk rock hair-dye,
electric sans-a-belt, god-awful golf-pants green.
Was it you? Was it you? I admit
chocolate chips were a reassuring if obvious brown
and, despite shapely suggestion of rat droppings,
I took my comfort there.

No Guts No Glory

Color coordinated refreshments
sustained us through the hot day
through dips in the pool
games of volleyball and croquet.
So I ate three slices of watermelon
bowl of blueberries with whipped cream
raspberries on a bed of angel food—
red M&Ms, blue Skittles,
and coconut jelly bellies by the handful,
two strawberry Daiquiris
four Piña Coladas
and a pitcher of tidy-bowl Margaritas.
Sara even infused the onion ring batter
with blue dye number seven,
adorned each platter with tiny bowls
of Tabasco and ranch dressing—
so crispy with pepper and salt,
I showed great restraint
only eating six greasy baskets full.
And let me tell you
while the others watched
fireworks decorate the lakeside night
and a brass band played
O'beautiful for spacious skies
a yankee-doodle do or die
from the redwood forest
to forever may she wave—
I never felt more patriotic
than kneeling on a red bathmat
beside the blue shower curtain
grasping white porcelain.

Ode to a Bartender

While recapping last night's highlights
the bartender poured a perfect stout
and when the door opened, we both
glanced above the bobbing, flirting heads.

Overdressed and a little too slim
almost boney with soft leathery wrinkles
and a golden-brown glow
like luggage I could not afford

she walked in tall and certain.
Kerry leaned across the bar,
Cancun my ass!
And I felt the setting of a trap—

now, is there some secret school
where they teach women how to glide
onto an empty barstool so their skirt
rides up just enough that you can't help

but glance and sigh? *Wanna buy me a drink?*
Danger, danger the red lights flashed
but I couldn't find my no
and that's when she earned her tip

I'm sorry sir, your credit card's been declined.
I stuffed a hundred dollar bill
into the jar beside the register, ducked out
the back door knowing I got away cheap.

Hazy with a Chance of ...   whatever

No idea
why I'm wearing
Hello Kitty boxer shorts
or how we
got from 6th street to the lake.
I remember quarter drafts
gave way to Goldschläger
and Kelly
flashed the bartender
for a round of Jello shots.
No, I don't
have any aspirin;
only solace
a shirt-pocket full
of empty condom foils.
On the bright side
our kisses don't taste
like vomit
and when you declared
Wow, what a night!
at least you were smiling.

Two Weeks in Rio

All my muses wear scarlet thongs
but only Terpsichore
spins so skirts flare high.
Salsa blares
as foolish feet pretend.
She places one hand on my left hip,
the other against my pelvis—
No, like this.

Oh yes, like that
and three days later I wake up
missing wallet and pubic hair—
spend the rest of my vacation
prowling dark streets
looking for a club nobody knows
listening for music I cannot dance.

A Note from the Clumsy Juggler #1

This is just to say
> I came quickly
> inside you
> and without
> a condom

> even though
> you made me
> promise
> to pullout in time.

> Forgive me
> you were drunk
> so willing
> and so gullible.

Benefits

We were never in red hearts and roses love—
in like and lonely more like it.
Tuesday nights became pizza and orgasms,
round-the-world weekends,
sleep late Sundays, naked pancakes
and if anyone asked, we'd say *just friends*.
Five or six months then one of us,
tapped by a stranger's stare, fell into their eyes.

In theory, either can call it off
for the real thing: no hard feelings,
still best buds, meet for lunch.
But it seems so selfish—fickle rainbow pursuit.
And now, every three months or so,
one of us wears a silly, no-reason grin.
Don't ask. Don't tell.
Just cross your fingers and hope it fails.

It Could Have Been Paris

and we could have been in love
but it was Fort Worth
and the breeze blew wisps of hair
across your forehead down into your eyes.
You brushed them back with a playful flip
while I recited lines by Millay—

very merry, back and forth all night upon the ferry.
You smiled and we sat comfortable
til the band played a fast polka and you took my hand.
We cha-cha'd with more abandon than skill

twisted as a hopeful moon slid past midnight,
waltzed that curves might be properly introduced.
As the band packed up guitars and drums and horns,
you kissed my forehead with the sweetest, sweetest
no.

So I went home and made love
in my tiny apartment on the Left Bank. After,
you smoked an unfiltered cigarette
while Edith Piaf sang *Danse Avec L'Amour
et Legionnaire's Regret.*

II. Busking

the poet like an acrobat climbs on rime
to a high wire of his own making
and balancing on eyebeams above a sea of faces
paces his way to the other side of day
—Lawrence Ferlinghetti

Busking

Sinking solstice sun and the clumsy juggler
breaks out fire sticks—bottles and joints
replace cans of Coke and Miller Lite.
Flames spinning above the boardwalk,
a night breeze, couples draw close.

Nicole stops by after her shift,
stays to watch blazing clubs rise
and fall and rise again. A fumbled catch,
shower of sparks, enthusiastic applause
and a satisfying toss of bills—
real danger was never the point.

Casual pecks ignite a crackling fuse.
Boom box beats, whirl of bodies sizzling—
maybe tonight she'll take him home.
Waves crash, moon and sirens rise.
Everything flashes, glows, screams or sings;
Welcome to the inferno where everyone
wants to burn.

Command Performance

bell cap
painted face white
patched silk blouse
tights
red diamond black

slight of pen
revealing rhymes
behind a princess ear
giggles of surprise

shiny balls and images
sent aloft
to fall in measured time
be caught
& quickly tossed again

laughter & applause

a promised tankard
of royal ale awaits

an ambitious conceit
or allegory
added to the whirl
spinning of delights

'til grace turns frantic
& a slighted beat
sends pretenses scattering

lips decurve
beneath jeweled crown
nods to bulging biceps
black-hooded head
over-expanded chest

& eager fingers
gliding over a blade
of glinting steel

Nicole Opens his Junk Drawer

I can explain
queen and jack of hearts missing from harlequin deck
warranty cards filled out with misplaced intentions
buttons never sewn back on
coffee-stained application to Barnum & Bailey school
ruby earrings never taken from their box
scattered dice and a rundown pocket watch

But don't ask about the red leather glove
postcards marked Cyprus, Beirut and Berlin
else I would have to explain one summer abroad
sticky nights filled with hash and ouzo
dominant blondes—salt rubbed wounds
cut of Mediterranean winds

The Clumsy Juggler Speaks
Directly into the Camera

I'm not very good at it—
could have been; came easy, keeping 4 or 5 balls aloft
but any more would have required practice
every day, and where's the fun in that?
And so what? Boardwalks aren't about skill
or even originality. I only have 4 routines—
variations from Lebowski's classic, *So You Want to
         Juggle.*

Boardwalks thrive on patter
and my tongue has always been more dexterous
than these hands.
So Dad, who used to bark a carnival,
taught me rhythm and projection.
Johnny Carson taught me to read the morning paper—
every fumbled catch, a political joke.
Particularly long routines called for an innuendo
about my sexual prowess.
Sometimes it was the other way around.

Obscure music references win over sullen teen,
huge tip if she smiles.
Whistle at the average looking women,
ask awesome babe's date if his mother
still dresses him (he knows she could do better—
tips large to prove he's cool).

And never ever let decibels fall—
chatter, joke, inquire. Observe, comment, and cajole.

Silence, the boardwalk's only sin
until that night Nicole kissed her fingers
and placed them firmly against my lips.

Black Ice

You and driving fast,
after three shots and a beer—
buzzing
winding through the hill country
feeling the rear end slip then catch.
Braking when radar detector tweets

waving to the cop
rounding the curve and gunning it.
Deer and low water crossings—
wooly-bully, wooly-bully—
topping a rise
missing a Harley head-on

and in the shadows
lurking during a mid-February cold snap
patches of black ice.
Yes, you and driving fast,
after three shots and a beer
are my two favorite things in the whole world.

A Note from the Clumsy Juggler #2

This is just to say
    I bought
    Bolshoi tickets
    with money
    from the lock box

    which you
    were probably saving
    to cover
    April's rent.

    Forgive me
    they leapt like gazelles
    so high
    and so filled with grace.

And What's Up With The Weather

Because rain falls sporadically and skies shift
    from light gray to dark
Because politicians hide in the restrooms
Because the greatest generation
    squandered all its chances
    and will not be given another
Because we dance to the talking heads
Because tourists expect to spend their dollars
Because my dad taught me to shoot a 22
Because winds finally deliver autumn to our doorstep
    and I do not wear sweaters
Because life and jazz both require improvisation
Because Walmart sells Guinness
    for 2 dollars less than my local market
Because what I believe doesn't change facts
Because Ray Bradbury says we should
    jump off cliffs all the time
Because the children of teen mothers
    spend more of their lives in prison and die earlier
Because twelve Senators gather for breakfast and prayer
Because Tony Romo can pass for 500 yards
    and the Cowboys will still find a way to lose
Because Archer Daniels Midland uses government
    subsidized grain to make high fructose corn syrup
Because I miss getting up a 5 a.m.
    to go fishing with my father
Because the president lunches with CEOs
    and the Koch brothers can give you
    70 billion very good reasons
Because geysers blow regardless of who isn't watching

Because human beings are animals
    evolved from other animals ad infinitum
Because every woman
    should have dominion over her own body
Because building wings is not so simple
    as writing a novel or launching a missile
Because the piano player
    launches into a slow Mood Indigo
Because abstinence is often more theory than fact
Because day or night the sun is still 93 million miles
    away
Because the confederate flag
    still flies over the old county courthouse
Because I believe the right to bear arms
    is almost as fundamental as free speech
Because they took down the painting of Luther Burbank
    spraying his field with Roundup
Because life is better with a syncopated beat
Because even blondes make jokes about our governor
Because I no longer eat meat and still love my country
Because the odds are always 5 to 4 against and Vegas
    makes money no matter which way you bet
Because icebergs are melting
Because Exxon Mobil receives
    over a billion dollars per year in corporate welfare
Because the bass player didn't get to sleep last night
Because our junior senator
    makes our governor look like a freak'n genius
Because smart is what we work to become,
    not something you were born with
Because two men can get married in New Mexico
    be arrested in Texas and killed in Nigeria
Because all privacy is illusion

Because weak-willed players
    cannot hit a softball question out of the infield
Because if I carried a gun,
    I'd take a shot at the SUV that just cut me off
Because scouts learn how to light a fire without a match
Because each year Halliburton spends over
    a million dollars on political donations and lobbying
Because shepherds watch for wolves
    and sheep need shearing in the spring
Because poll results do not change facts
Because nobody should have to choose between
    going to the doctor and paying their electric bill
Because day or night
    the sun is only 93 million miles away
Because I no longer hunt or fish
Because the smartest teenagers will do
    the dumbest things and the off switch is broken
Because the Attorney General says
    we don't really do that anymore
Because the earth used to be flat
Because barbequed tofu
    will never taste like great barbeque
Because stained glass hides what is on the other side
Because clocks do not all tick the same
    and Schrodinger never placed a cat in a box
Because every year, somewhere,
    the leaves turn gold and red
Because congress will screw it up
    again and again and again
The sax player launches into a another solo
    reaching for something beyond
    and must fail else never play again.

The Worst Cup of Coffee in the World

Jimmy Whitefish gets up a 5 a.m.,
plugs in the Brewmaster 4000,
and while the chrome pot percolates,
he pounds sign into sand—
Stop!
The World's Worst Coffee!
Free Inside!

And they do, and it is—
bitter as his cousin's Vietnam stories,
lukewarm just like the way his son says *uh-huh, yeah,*
okay. And as the day wears on,
java thickens like his father's slurred denials.
Regulars know you can add sugar, milk, or creamer
but it never gets any better, just different.

Once a bored busker asked,
     What do you do for a living?
Isn't it obvious?
I make the world's worst coffee.
     No, really, how do you make money?
and Jimmy just stares back
as if he doesn't understand the question.

Circling the Mallard Pond
for Mary Oliver

Mary kneels in the rough grass,
her angular face a glory of attention focused
on the praying mantis crossing her forearm.
We are on the path where it circles the old mallard pond
(a shortcut to the library)
and though I began in solitude, choose to walk
the rustling, twittering, sloshing silence
with my companion of chance.

I point to the top of a rusty pine
where a Red-shouldered Hawk surveys
the evening landscape—a tempest of crows
clatters about like falling bones
til our vigilant guardian rises in irritation,
disappears among the tangled treetops.
Mary is perceptive and bold as fantasy invites me
to share my new poem, listens intently
as I speak of turtles, raptors and an unclouded heart.

When we reach the old dock, Mary begins her verse:
another pond, unnamed, where sun sets
and spreading egret wings placed in measured lines
challenge us to find our own reflection.
We pause at a rush of cattails and Mary confesses
her inspiration was a sunrise and scattering of coots.

It seems but a few steps
before the trail forks. My books are overdue,
so I bear left into town
while Mary continues down along the water's edge.

Walking with Monet

through a grove of olive trees
to a pebbled Mediterranean shore
where the painter asked what I had seen—
to describe light falling through leaves,
illuminated undergrowth.

Claude removed his shoes
and rolled up baggy trouser legs,
splashed in the surf
'til I trailed off my failure complete.
Then he told the tale of Joseph
humble cobbler who went blind
trying to answer the same question.

Finally I told him about a time
when I was 12 years old and picked
all the dandelions in our yard.
Unsatisfied, I gathered dogwood petals
high as I could reach,
freed my mother's garden
of iris and azalea blooms,
misted the pile with lighter fluid
and set the blossoms ablaze.

It was more beautiful, more beautiful
more beautiful
and only because no one ever asked
more beautiful than what.

On Becoming the Best Poet in the Room

After shooting Billy Collins
I took his last cannoli
out of the oven
and left it to cool
by an open window
while wondering
what to do about Mary Oliver?

Flashlight Starchild Connexion

Bernie and Bootsy launched into *Aqua Boogie*,
Sir Bignose passing round doobies from the crowd
while Grandpa George, wearing rainbow pajamas,
took it all in—arms spread in some metaphysical hug.
Miss. Karen kissed me with promise,
and any difference between walking and dancing
had long since disappeared.

That's when the Mother Ship landed. Right in the middle
of Golden Gate Park. Well, it didn't really land,
but a billion flashing lights put the bay night to shame
and hovered maybe 20 feet above our heads. Dozens
of ramps descended; band climbed on board, crowd
let out a cheer, and one hundred thousand
funk monsters joined the ultimate trip.
Less than an hour later
ramps retract, and the Mother Ship launched itself
back toward the stars.

There might have been a hundred of us left
wandering the littered grounds.

Now, P-Funk had disappeared before, but they never
took so many fellow funksters along, and this time
there wouldn't be any reunion tour.
Nobody really made a big deal out of it—thirty seconds
on *Entertainment Tonight*, half-page with photo
in *Rolling Stone*. Friends and families gave
most of their stuff away—look,
I got Henry and Maurice's 52 inch plasma TV.

All-in-all, life goes on pretty much as before,
except I tell this story every year when my freshman read
The Road Not Taken. To their clamoring why,
the best I can say is that I did not hear the call.

Remembering The King of Pop

Clair and I sang *ABC* and took second place
in the Green Valley Middle School Talent contest.
What the judges never understood
is that we were imitating Captain and Tennille.
Later we slow danced to *Ben* (Mom wouldn't let me see
any movie starring a rat), and Clair rested her hand
on my butt. I was too nervous to return the favor.

We thought any guy that sang *Rockin Robin*
had to be gay, but loved the Robot. Nobody asked how
someone so cool invented
the ultimate geeky white boy dance. I was scarecrow,
and Clair played Dorothy in our high school's
all white production of *The Wiz*.

Spent three months learning to moonwalk, practiced
like Tom Cruise in Risky Business, tried it out
at The Black Light, and nobody even noticed.
I was probably the only one who went home alone,
and *Beat It* became just another hairy palm joke.

Painted Jackie, Tito, Jermaine, Marlon, and Michael
on my clubs, and with *I'll Be There* on the boom box,
struggling to keep all the clubs aloft, I let the crowd
go wild guessing which brother tumbled first.
Somebody always got a laugh asking about Randy.

In retrospect, Jacko should never have been allowed
to sing *we are the children*, needed to work on his tan,
and surely Lisa Marie could've done better.
But know what? Whenever I gotta drive all night,

I still put *Thriller* and *Billy Jean* on the playlist,
always sing along because I still know all the words.

The Clumsy Juggler at the Crossroads

Juggler needed
to keep people and plans in the air
Bored imp placed the ad,
salary more than I would make
in a summer's worth of boardwalk summers.
Sulfurous breath blew discarded page
against my trunk. Nicole laughed,
dared me and on a lark
I borrowed her brother's suit.

Hell of it is
I'm a much better operations manager
than surfside busker. At my desk,
in my cube, typing, clicking,
staring at the screen—I never
lose track of any resource, deadline,
project. In meetings I wax eloquent
throw around tactical and strategic goals,
allocations, pie charts, cost controls.

And just for a salt-in-the-wound laugh
horned-boss gives me a promotion,
a raise, a window I can stare out
thirty floors above the boardwalk.

Kryptonite

Superman wants to write a teen novel—
inspirational tale of a boy wizard
who when bitten by a dragon
loses his ability to make magic—
but every time he sits down at his computer
some airplane stalls over the arctic
or a bridge collapses with a school bus
teetering on the brink.

Clark Kent paid a seven hundred
and fifty-four dollar penalty when
on April 15th at 11:45 p.m.
a magnitude 7.2 quake
sent a tsunami Metropolis way.

Lois complains that he never calls
only spend time together
when she's dangling from a skyscraper,
suggested a week off
maybe a Jamaican cruise
like that's ever gonna happen.

Perry's on his case for another scoop
something to send papers
flying off the stands. Circulation's falling.
Jimmy Olsen laid off
and now he has to take his own photographs,
stays up worrying
how he'll pay the rent if the Planet folds.

Superman still hasn't seen
the final episode of the Sopranos
or read the Franzen novel
gathering dust beside his La-Z-Boy.
Lately he's popping
superhuman doses of Rolaids and Prilosec,
blood pressure's higher than that stoner Mxyzptlk.
Even Lex Luther is beginning to worry
suggested he switch to decaf
maybe smoke a little herb.

Crossing the North Quad

She walks across the lawn,
a smooth glimpse casually given

teenage cotton and tan lines
exchanged for a live beat.

Tonight after she swallows
her last bite of pizza

she'll tell roommates it was a leer.
Gross and giggles and just maybe

give I was once nineteen,
rock-hard and broke,

but no way grok
how pale florescent days

leave a permanent squint,
years just more pounds to shed,

that desire grows
in creek-side brambles

free to pick
if you don't mind thorns,

purple lips,
sticky-sweet down your chin.

Some Mornings

it might be Monday or the kids
screaming
maybe a hangover
or eight hours typing on the screen
whatever
some mornings you cannot find
a reason why
and so shrink away as sunbeams
pierce the window
pull covers over your head
and return to a dream
of flying goatmen and daffodil rain
of laughter
and a ticking that never stops
until escape
back to that world
ruled by alarm clocks and gravity
becomes a treasure map
locked away
until even the prick of fresh coffee
with bacon frying
cannot trip the tumblers
until the heart surrenders
and the rats finally have their day.

The Aerialist

In 1897, Jules Leotard introduced
a new act to his Cirque de Fantastique

Letting go, the bar swings away
and she becomes just one more subject
of gravity, momentum, karma
and the best she can do is spin and stretch.

The tape (all aerialists have a copy)
shows the great falls—Mexico City 1931,
Alfredo Codona slips from his brother's grasp.
Detroit 1962, Wallenda Pyramid collapses.
Paris 1954, The Amazing Van der Wertz
inexplicably releases on the back swing
lands in the crowd,
kills self and a 6 year old boy.

Real trapeze artists do not pray (their glory
is not God's) nor do they believe in the net—
only will and hubris
enable this unnatural act. Her only thought,
while hanging suspended in our awe,
is that her leotard
sparkles like a young girl's dream.

Cube Dweller Confession

I don't mind the blood so much
but cracking sound as axe splits our boss's skull
keeps that from being my favorite workplace fantasy
(drops it to number four,
between stock split and copier that never jams).
No, my favorite begins with the getaway—
leaving his crumpled body,
feeling a tad sorry for putout cleaning crew,
hijacking corporate jet
parachuting into some Caribbean paradise
that never heard of extradition,
where rum drinks are sweet and fruity
and served by pliant women
wearing nearly sufficient bikinis.
But the best part is every year on the anniversary
I toast his ghost and read sacks of email—
former coworkers singing praises to my name.

Every Spring

ecstatic dandelions
sprout and bloom and puff
rulers of the unmowed field
and we feel the pull
of goofy grin sweaty palms
pounding heart.
After all no rational person truly believes
in the one and only soul mate.
Thunder bellows
then rain drenches the eager grass
and we might strip off our clothes
to spin free, except we understand
it's all chemical,
phenylethylamine and oxytocin,
that the real thing is built over seasons
brick by experienced brick
so we sit by the window and watch
the lightning flash
sip our hot black coffees
and have to talk about it.
If nobody believes in one and only
why can't we throw up our hands and trust
the humid promise of spice
and palm and a nodding moon.
After all there must be any number of people
right for me and right for you
at least until I met you
you met me and we
embraced inevitable loss—
until all the others begin to fade
seeming, in the end, slightly absurd.

The Tinker and the Bard
for Jack Hardy

Wandering fire to fire, night to day to night,
spinning songs on a black guitar—
the tinker and the bard
seeking the good goat call down the moon.
Like a snake in the rye grass uncertain of his venom,
the tinker and the bard whisper lies
we gather like unpolished gems,
plant grapes for someone else to harvest.
Bastard tinker, dancing bard
watch the lightning flash, the water rise,
a maypole anchor beneath the Coho tarp.
Worshiping, cursing, the tinker and the bard
believe each muse their due,
listen for the cuckoo's coo,
poke fun at the politicians, shine a light in the rectory,
and realizing there is nothing they can do
answer yes when the jester calls.
The tinker and the bard arrive in a green Studebaker
drink your whiskey and your beer,
leave forget-me-nots on the bedside table
and before the dawn, disappear.

Smoke Signals

A Man knocks on my door and wants to come in. I say no, it is too hot and he goes away.

A Man knocks on my door and wants to give me a painting of Che Guevara. We hang it above the fireplace and he goes away.

A Man knocks on my door and wants to give me his sister. I tell him she is too young and he goes away.

A Man knocks on my door and wants to replace Che with a statue of Cesar Chevez. I say no and he lands a punch and goes away.

A Man knocks on my door and wants to give me 2 extra-strength capsules. I swallow; my jaw still hurts and he goes away.

A Man knocks on my door and wants to burn my house down. I ask him to come back later and he goes away.

A Man knocks on my door and wants to give me a hug, is too embarrassed and he goes away.

A Man knocks on my door and wants to read me his manifesto. I offer him money but he continues to read. Finally I close the door and hope he goes away.

A Man knocks on my door and wants to share his gin and tonics. We talk of fishing and football. He does not like the painting of Che and he goes away.

A Man knocks on my door and wants to burn my house down. I say why not. Firemen laugh at the flames and he goes away.

A Man knocks on my door and wants to read what I have written. I ask him if he is my father and he goes away.

After Nicole

The thing life teaches you is that people die.
One day you're in your favorite restaurant
sharing pad-Thai, tofu satay, wide noodles with
        jalapenos,
and the next you're deciding between caskets and
        cremation.
When's the memorial service? Don't send flowers.

Plane tickets and making sure the cats get fed,
answering *what happened* over and over and over
til it drones out like a mantra. Saying thank you
for casseroles, and loaves of fresh bread. Saying thank
        you
just when you think you'll never feel like eating again.
Her best friend is out-of-town 'til Saturday.
Who else did I forget to call?

That's her Mother on the phone and she won't stop
        crying.
I don't know what to say; we never got along
that well when her daughter was alive and this intimacy
is too awkward now. *Suit clean? Shoes shined?*
Which shirt? Which tie? Pants too tight. I need a
        haircut.

And then it's over. People start to leave you alone again.
Each day fewer cards mixed in with her magazines,
the bills and ads. Each day fewer of those calls,
mumbling, embarrassed, *I'm so sorry I hadn't heard.*
Only close friends still ask *how's it going.*

Thank you notes get written. Work becomes busy.
Six months pass.

And then one day you're driving nowhere in particular
when a song comes on the radio (not any special song,
but just some song). You have to pull over, sob out
the knot in your gut. And only because you can't stay
on the shoulder forever, you crank the car back up,
pull out into traffic and choose which way to go.

After Indigo

No one knows why the tiger came inside.
There had been reports, orange and black,
ever since Indigo died and we had generously ignored
the occasional chicken or goat gone missing.
But here it is, stretched-out across my kitchen table,
head nested in crook-crossed paws—
eyes neither menacing nor curious,
neither innocent nor wise,
but calm and lively like a tiny miracle,
a turned maple leaf swirling into your breast pocket.

The stock has been fed, yard scoured
for fresh laid eggs. Sensuous,
the coffee waits to be poured,
mug filled, newspaper read. Instead I sit,
idly scratch behind a twitching ear,
accept rumbling purr as encouragement.
Sandpaper tongue laps over a lazy morning's stubble,
rubs temple and ear a raw, vigorous red.
Too soon the nannies will cry for their milking.

I do not leave doors open
and all the windows have screens.
This is unimportant;
she moves to her own tick and turn.
I wake to find her sprawled across my chest,
half-nestled beneath the blanket, wonder
so many pounds can insinuate without disturbance.
I see her while picking beans,
a languid silhouette edging the field.

I dive into the creek where it widens into a deep pool
and when I break the surface she is paddling along side.

Copernicus Sits at His Desk
Explaining to Atropos

how our spinning jigsaw puzzle
with its too many pieces
its constant shift and roil
rises in the Martian sky
brightest star in retrograde

unwilling to follow the prescribed arcs
a flaw
in the elliptical dance of glimmering cousins

we turn back
as if we've forgotten our luggage
heavy with cosmic effluvia
accumulations named necessity and desire

of course we have always been wanderers

the equations which predict our return
require a translation of coordinates
moving the origin
toward a more honest center

and the best hope
is that no great levers become unbalanced
by a twinkle-twinkle starlight prayer
mumbled
upon our first appearance in the night.

So This Is Falling

Temptation wears a blue tank top, no bra, keeps blond
       hair
bleached white, cropped short and spiky.

Barely half my age, everything she does—
the way she laces pink chucks, plops down on a beanbag
       chair,

peels a Clementine—everything pulses like spring tides.
Paperback in the pocket of her 501s,

Temptation reads Whitman, Nin, *Zen and the Art
of Motorcycle Maintenance*, rides a yellow Vespa

to her job at the coffee bar—never naïve, she still
       believes
in organic vegetables, tossed out her television.

Wild like laughter, when we kiss, she tends to bite,
so I tend to bleed. Temptation is the long step from the
       cliff top.

On the way down God winks at me, but I do not cry out—
my only hope lies off the rocks, lost at sea.

Autumn Leaves, Winter Frost
& an Electric-blue Dildo

Like that copy of Ulysses so casually displayed,
its presence the unspoken lie

So long, so thick—sure to intimidate anyone
wanting just a little something to read

You complained that I've never written you a poem,
called upon Erato and compared you to pearls or gold

I always loved how your hair smelled like lemon pledge

And now I dedicate my poems
to the muse of hair shirts and frustration

In a shadow cast by the old oak
moonlight filtered through the frosty window

you can see our initials engraved in laughter's
                condensation
Of course that was last fall before trees turned rust;

it's winter now; I've raked the fallen leaves
and it's past time to clean that window.

Visiting Connecticut
and Reading Mary Oliver

My nylon jacket is zipped against the breeze.

I walk beside abandoned tracks
cutting through the shaded forest
til rails dive beneath the surface
of a small nameless pond.
In a few months skaters will twirl and waltz
but today the sun still answers yes
so I sit on a sycamore's mossy lawn
shifting 'til my back finds comfortable purchase

pull apart the deep green covers to read
about a bear in spring looking down a hill
and right there near the middle of the page
she writes *there is only one question,*
how to love this world. Juggler,
how do you love this world?

A blue heron poses
with neck and bill arching toward a shallow.
Its new winter coat is as dark and navy
as my windbreaker. In my wonder
grip on place and binding slip away.
Mischievous zephyrs
do not miss such opportunities,
leaves turn and Mary says to me
you finally knew what you had to do, and began.
But I do not know. How can I know? I am deaf
to the spare patches of red and gold whispering
turn, turn and let go.

I know these clothes weigh too much
so I leave them to rot beneath soon fallen leaves,
wade into the refreshing chill
and choose a gentle breaststroke
for my crossing. A too kind
or perhaps absent minded friend
has left a freshly laundered towel
on the opposite shore and I dry myself.
Up the grassy slope
a wooden cabin waits with open door.
A bowl of fresh-picked raspberries
sits as a still life on the rough-hewn table.
They are delicious.

Perhaps, after the sun has descended
a pair of hopeful young bodies
will find her words and my clothes
discarded beside the abandoned rails.
She will try on the blue windbreaker,
find it too large but comforting.
The moon will be bright enough
so he will read to her
Don't bother me
I've just been born
and they will both know it is true.
He will read to her about two women
meeting in the Singapore airport
and they will look around for birds.

Finally they will shed their clothes
and swim out
where their feet cannot touch bottom.
She will kiss him on the cheek

and he will brush his pale blue lips
to her forehead and they will both know
it is not their time to swim across.
She will wear the jacket home
and he will carry the words
tucked between his elbow and ribs.

The Clumsy Juggler Considers Suicide

It's never about the destination

Doors, desks, and plexiglass panes—
sit here, look there, more walls and tables,
more chairs industrial beige
until you reach the end of the hall
where the elevator waits to take you up or down.

But I am the heretic smashing sheetrock,
crawl between walls, follow pipes and wires,
watch what flows in and out unseen,
grab a forgotten wrench, pound a window
til the shatterproof shatters,
leap thirty floors above the street.

Yeah, landing could be hell,
but what a fall—four seconds of wind and gravity
and perhaps never meeting the pavement.
Grab hold of some feathered hope,
drop to a slanted roof.
And so what if concrete is terminal,
only hobgoblins require doors and walls.
Neither fire nor love—neither basement nor clouds.
And that's okay too.

III. Taking a Bow

It was worth death to see you through these optic nerves,
To feel breeze through the fur on my arms
To be chilled and stirred in your mortal martini.
—Tony Hoagland

Epiphany

The day after
the tree had been sent to mulch
last turkey sandwich eaten, gift exchanged
last party over, relative gone
bowl game won and lost

the day after it was finished
it finally arrives.

I find myself humming
a song about the birth of a child,
a child of light to balance the dark

feel joy
and relief the joy still comes.

My thoughts drift to an ancient wanderer
forced to travel on winter's eve
catching sight of Saturnalia fires
burning in a distant time's square
fighting the encroaching darkness
willing the sun to return

I get it—
even if I don't light any candles
don't dance and shout with tinseled glee,
if I sit in silence
bathed in the holiness of long dark nights,
the light will still return.

Today

Today I will surrender needles and razor blades—
speak nothing but truth, I will declare love
or not and will not know which until it is too late.
I will grab the dragon's neck, swing onto her back,
ride until consumed by the sun.
I will climb gasping from of the surf
all flesh and kelp and desire.
And if my heel lands on a sharpened shard,
I will wince and bleed and bind the wound.

Pendulum and Nightfall: A Love Poem

*A man is rich in proportion to the number
of things which he can afford to let alone.*
　　　　　　　　—Henry David Thoreau

My heart stopped
startled by the first tap of the hung over
day after Mardi Gras dawn
as if beating were some trivial luxury like caffeine,
like beer, like chocolate
surrendered forty days in anticipation.

A passionless shell, deaf to pendulum and nightfall,
I rail at the evening news and quote Thoreau.
Unread magazines wait for recycling.

Come Halloween, I opened my door to goblins,
pirates, anime heroes and wart-nosed witches. You
mad-doctor instantly diagnosed
and plunged your scalpel into my chest,
spread these brittle ribs.
You reached inside and pulled out a withered mass—
empty chambers and lazy valves.
Undeterred, you squeezed,
released and squeezed again, and again

until some pale memory fired.
Crude stitches, leaky veins, shallow breath,
and somebody to tell the difference
if and when I die.

Texas Sun Poem

Yes, come mid-winter, I'll sing and dance and beg
his return, but this is the fifth straight triple digit day.
Sign on the corner reads one-o-six. Hell
it was eighty-four degrees when I stepped
outside this morning. *Ice on Bridge* my ass.

Yes, when the night falls early, I'll sing and dance
and beg his return, but the best I can offer
this blazing sky is a middle finger salute—sun dial
        shadow
pointing across black tar parking lot
where my car waits baking.

Yes, when weathermen calculate wind chill, I'll sing
and dance and beg his return, but today the humidity
could drown a fish. Windows down. AC on turbo blast.
Steering wheel too hot to touch. Give me a break.

Give me an ice cold Shiner, bucket of Blue Bell,
give me a dip in the Brazos. Give me your parking place
in the shade and I'll tell you a secret. It doesn't matter
if we sing and dance and beg, not really, because the sun
doesn't care. The sun only knows how to rise and set.
The sun just burns.

When I Jumped the Curb

bounced my El Camino through a hedge of azaleas
shattered plate glass, parked in your sunroom—
you opened the door, offered me your hand
asked if I would like a slice of chocolate or raspberry
       torte.

So we spend an afternoon chattering whyfore and
       wherenot
arrival of warm fronts, late blooming dogwood
death of an underappreciated musician.
And somewhere a jazz combo plays standards

we both recognize yet are unable to name.
Three deer wander in from the woods
grazing upon acorn and buttercup. Fading twilight
leaves us beneath a moonless, cloudless, starless sky

and there is nothing else in the whole world
except two people sitting at a solid oak table
two people slightly less frightened than curious
two people drinking sweet wine into the night.

Riddle

The first time I came to dinner, her 15-year-old daughter
looked me in the eye and asked, *So what is god?*

I paused then said, god is losing your balance and the
        library after midnight. Yard work blisters and the
        deepest snow in 50 years. Tripping down the
        stairs and peeling your first Clementine.

Tumbling in a wave, your body stretching out of
        childhood, Rubenesque cherries, Cajun dancing,
        and the one time you do exactly what your
        mother asks.

Bleeding from a wound, matching every Tupperware
        bowl to its lid, rent coming due. And finally,
        without which I could not go on, faith in one
        more great book to read.

Then she turned to her mother and with a forkful of
        spaghetti said, *Oh yeah, this one's a real keeper.*

sticky guilt: a tale of two strawberries

house-robed and barefoot
I rush past the wild lawn
to our garden where
sometime in the brief night
a multitude of fragile iris
found courage to bloom
and there waiting
beneath an overhanging
and dew-slick leaf
having escaped mite and mold
and sharp-eyed jay
two perfect strawberries

this is already too much
to ask of a refulgent spring
but look here
those pale blue flowers
foretell baskets
filled with peas and beans
these towering stalks
promise sweet
sweet corn
bounty of our clumsy labor
piled high
in the old red wagon

remember that chilly afternoon
turning the soil
with buckets of sheep manure
from your uncle's farm
planting a ring of spearmint

to deter curious deer
and how later we
stripped off
muddy jeans and flannel shirts
sprayed one another
with the hose
then tumbled laughing
back into the wet dirt

you will admire
how the blue vase
(the one you bought
at the gallery opening)
sets off red and purple petals
and I will hand you
a mug of rich jasmine tea
with plenty of lemon
and before taking a sip
you will taste
sweet fruit on my lips
then lick the sticky guilt
still lingering on my cheek

The Last Entry of a Minor Functionary

In the year of our Lord
one thousand seven hundred eighty-nine
on the eleventh glorious day
of the auspicious month of September:
 of course they wanted our heads.

We ate succulent pig
and swilled the most expensive wines,
amused ourselves with fine trinkets
of silver and porcelain while hunger like a cutthroat
lurking in a darkened alley
passes unseen by gendarmes
and taxmen bold on the streets.

I thought I might escape
with my own cranium still attached. After all,
I lived on the outskirts of town,
had hoped the mobs would spend coins of rage
at gaudier markets near the palace.
My family's name was never common
with society's gossips.

And really I was not so immodest as all that,
skimmed no more than expected, too busy
keeping my wife presentably attired, sons out of trouble,
negotiating husbands for finicky daughters.
Extravagance was not our style, but unavoidable
burden of birth.

Perhaps I would be given an opportunity
to renounce dear Marie

to surrender all our worldly goods and allowed
the redemption of honest work,
but boiling pots of discontent
chose to overflow as I was delivering
some quickly irrelevant proclamation to the court.

Now revolution
does not change the plight of men and women.
There will always be those who live
by more than their share and necks like ours,
scrubbed clean beneath delicate lace collars
never more than a toss of coins
from being laid upon the block.

Liberty After Midnight

September 11, 2003

Where is she going in her top-down Thunderbird?
I bet she's older than she looks
but younger than the classic she drives. And who waits
to greet, or question, or scold?

Perhaps her lover (a man or a woman?)
watches her step from the blue convertible,
pours steaming tea and leaves
the white china cups to cool. They kiss
and she unties her red scarf—a knot of lilacs
in a tall ceramic vase rising as expectations,
as a flame from her torch.

Perhaps the band segues from *Lady
Be Good* into a slow *Mood Indigo*
and the bartender fixes her gin with a twist.
She waits until her drink is half empty,
the melody come and gone, steps to the microphone,
blue eyes on a stranger against the bar.

Nothing holds like the shore
when the moon begins to fall.

Perhaps she discards her sandals and the hem
of her skirt grows wet. She watches
the pale dawn reclaiming a once blackened horizon,
forgets what happened that September, spots
a sand dollar as the waves recede.

She will have the bleached disk crafted into a pendant,
tuck it in the back of her jewelry box,
velvet wrapped and never worn.

meditation on an independent day

exploding sky, exploding man
field, mountain, desert
shock and awe, shock and awe
street, market, hotel
rocket's red glare, rocket's red glare
bodies, cameras, wailing

exploding sky, shock and aaah
laughter, symphony, applause
exploding woman, rocket's red glare
hot dogs, watermelon, beer
shock and awe, spacious skies
exploding children, land that I love

Returning to Columbia

February 1, 2003

Forty miles and the tug is palpable
drawn toward the inevitable
hug of an anxious wife, eager kids,
congratulatory toasts of champagne
'til adrenaline drains away, invites
a deep satisfying sleep.
Cloudless, the dawn affirms
each long night will turn,
hopeful the center line stretches
an invitation down the blacktop.

But time has a way of bending
back upon itself.
Nearly forgotten, the weaver sits
on some distant hill, bent to her loom,
barely aware of the design.
Songs on the radio do not segue
one oldies hit to the next,
flow broken by somber reports—
DJ names a shuttle fallen,
seven travelers lost to home.

The cab shakes with each imperfection
dropped, blown or poured into the pavement.
Curves are obscured by a settling fog.
I ease off the gas, tighten
my grip on the wheel, lean slightly forward,
fully awake for those final miles.

All That Remains

Line by line in time, adding up the cost,
picking at charred, still smoldering remains,
counting the turned and broken things I've lost.

Scorched photographs, a chair, our bed burned dross—
two lives summed as ash. Filling out the forms
line by line in time, adding up the cost.

Walls repel—shattered panes invite the frost.
Pale memories summon misty night fumes
to count each turned and broken thing. I've lost

my way; familiar streets no longer cross.
I am wordless, crumpling pages once groomed
line by line. In time, adding up the cost

is more burden than it's worth. But chaos
fades, I recall your passing as a storm
do not count you a broken thing I've lost.

I pray like fire reaches for air, not chance.
Black grace is the final ledger's balance.
Line by line in time, adding up the cost—
counting all turned and broken things we've lost.

The Clumsy Juggler
Returns to the Boardwalk

Noisy mime winks at cute blonde.
Two break dancers spin on a red mat.
Strung-out guitarist sings another Beatles' song.

I love the salty, humid breeze
and how everyone gives up on their hair.

Roller Blades dodge amorous couples,
joggers jogging and toddling toddlers,
dogs straining at their leash.

I feel for trampled sand,
envy arrogance and freedom of waves.

Onions fry—scent mingled
with burgers, potatoes, and funnel cake.
Squawking gulls seek unguarded treats,
beg for stale bits of bun and pizza crust.

I have half a sand dollar in my pocket,
broken shells and a pretty piece of driftwood.

Clusters of tweenage girls giggle—older sisters
seeking shadow kisses. Boys, not quite so clueless
as they seem, jostle, leap and laugh too loud.

I was never so young, but seem to recall
swimming with dolphins and sharks.

Crumpled wrappers climb out of overflowing barrels
scale clap-board stands.

I step off the boardwalk, head down the beach
toward a setting sun and tidal pools.

Unlike Robert Haas, I never used the word *blackberry* in a poem

but still grok the stickiness and the purple,
desire and thorn-drawn beads of blood.
Unlike Will Rogers, I never typed
a newspaper column while flying in a biplane,
but I've felt the engine stall and watched the earth
hurdling upward. And unlike Georgia O'Keefe,
I never posed in a dingy New York apartment,
but I've woken naked in the desert
and seen sunrises through bleached-out pelvic bones.
I've taken the final shot, then stood frozen
like a ball hanging on the rim, and I've slept on the sofa
when unwelcome in my own bed.
Unlike Bill Evans, I never shot-up in a Paris step-down,
but I still grok the stickiness and the purple,
ennui and tiny beads of blood. And unlike Quentin Crisp,
I never defended my life before the magistrate,
just pled guilty and paid fines that left me gasping,
and with all the new talk about loss
still found time to scoop homemade ice cream
into bowls of steaming cobbler.

Beneath a Voyeur Moon

Too early to be late
but late enough the neighborhood
has found its way to bed

and cool enough for two old night owls
to sit on the front porch
not talking about that other thing

when the slow dance
from my junior prom comes drifting
through an open window.

Hand-in-hand we walk
out into the lane, step shuffle
and turn along the dashed white line

neither leading nor being led
eyes in eyes, steal a kiss
sweet with coffee and chocolate

hands roaming ribs to thighs
keeping time to the heady scent
of magnolia and melody

I don't know how they know to look
but up and down the lane
curtains twitch

children peek and giggle
at those two old people pretending
forgetting age and propriety

the same way you giggled
spying on your sister and her date
home on time

hip-to-hip on the swing
before finally saying good night.

Some Lines I was Working on When I Heard the News

Silly spring
laughing
as if another drunken sunset
tumbling
like an avalanche of peaches
into a sea of nectar
could erase
 words from memory.

Silly spring
laughing
as shirtless boys
swing from knotty vines
and dive into the chill stream—
every mother knowing
the swift current waits
to pull you under
and never let go.

Silly spring
laughing
as if preachers
do not own their Sunday mornings—
sure, we can still spin and jitterbug
past midnight
but strawberry tarts
cooling on the windowsill
will never taste so sweet again.

The Last Day of March

I woke with an unfettered morning
dressed in a long-sleeved t-shirt and my old blue jeans
laced boots, grabbed binoculars
and headed for the park
just like I had done so many other mornings.
Through patchy clouds and a light fog
birds chattered and chirped,
flit from brush to bush to leafed-out branch.
I duly noted a low-flying marsh-hawk
and gaudy cardinals
flirting as if it were the second week of spring.
I peered into the thick tangle
looking for the short, notched tail
that distinguishes savannah sparrow from song,
prowled thicket for towhee and thrasher.
As the sun began to burn through
blue birds emerged from their boxes
and the air was filled with swift and swallow
darting and diving over the field.
For three hours 'til an upstart
with chestnut back and white eyebrow
hops onto a rotting log and calls
empty-camp, isn't it, isn't it—
empty-camp, isn't it, isn't it—
for three hours I did not think
of Michael, or Jack, or Ed,
but now all I can do is glare and remember
and finally
when this silence cannot stand any longer
I yell fuck you.

A nearby jogger hurries on,
empty-camp, isn't it, isn't it—
and the tiny wren vanishes into the reeds.

Eagle Scout Project

Brent from Troop 753
built these benches along the Bittern Trail
so I might pause
where the rare-glimpsed beavers lodge and mask-faced
wood ducks swim.

And he carved
the words of Wendell Berry on a wooded plank
so I might find
the peace of wild things in the still water
and vibrant chickadees.

A flitting marsh wren
lands beneath the bench and pecks at my bootlace
as if I belonged in this swamp
where forethought is a stranger
and mournful cries subsumed by need.

I do not claim brotherhood with the sulking coyote, ever
alert deer or passing bobcat, but perhaps this winter day
they recognize something untamed that does not disturb
the blue heron nor rustle the brown-stemmed reeds.

Black and white ducks
arc low to land with a brief splash
and swim among the lily pads
but I will not lift these binoculars
nor search my pockets for their name.

Last Snow

No child—it doesn't snow, not here, not really,
only occasional flurries
destined to melt in a dull afternoon sun.
But once—and surely you are too young to remember
when Lupe with her beautiful swollen belly
rode one of Ramon's donkeys
along the candle lit streets.
As they turned onto Plaza del San Francisco
toward the old mission square,
the sky blossomed with airy white flakes.
All the children sang *Welcome O Virgin, Mother of God.*
And I think it was your very grandmother
who sang the *Ave Maria*
as Father Antonio opened the chapel door.
After mass, we did not rush home
in the clatter of expectant children,
but someone opened a cask of wine and somebody else
produced a candied cake.
There were tamales and crème-filled rolls,
and Sister Theresa played the old songs. The youngest,
covered in fatherly coats, fell asleep on the pews.
And when we could no longer deny the morning,
we walked out into blinding radiance—
snow deeper than these boots.

Museuming With Mom

My mother sits besides the stage
in Romare Bearden's *Midnight Jam*—
she and her college roommate flirting
with two young men who buy the drinks.

In the Calder mobile my mom is a curved blade
painted royal and glossy blue.
Dangling from a thin line, she slowly pivots
 as everything rotates off center.

She walks with one of Giacometti's striding men,
and loses herself in Monet's garden,
does not appear in old Dutch Masters
but with an easy precision explains how and why
of illuminated faces. Standing before
a pair of Rembrandts she notes the grimy urchin
and patrician lady stare out of identical gray eyes.

In Thomas Eakins' *Swimming Hole*, she is
a young girl spying on brothers she never had.
And there in Ansel Adams' *Wagons
by the Yellowstone River*—perfectly focused
but too small to see—she rides in the buckboard,
blonde-haired girl practicing her stitchery.

Then we are back at the Bearden
only this time she is older, sitting with my father
drinking gin and quietly singing the lyrics
to every slow and burning song.

when you lose the keys

and directions to the grocery store become a spaghetti
of turn left yield next right circle back nowhere

when the recipe on a box of mix leaves you crying
and you cannot remember if that orange light
means the stove is on or off

when you lose za and qi and xi
and none of the seven letter words you taught me
fit on your scrabble board

when you lose steinbeck and hemingway
faulkner and wolfe and welty melt
like ink on a soggy page

when you stumble over stardust
skylark and it's only a paper moon

when dim lit suitors come unmoored in time
and even when you lose my name
in a clatter of grandchildren

on a ripe june morning i will pick a fragrant bucket full
then with ella on the turntable serve you
chilled strawberries with warm biscuits
and fresh whipped cream.

Dixon

When the singer locked eyes with mine
I saw him forget the words
and it wasn't love or desire
but the way I forget the color of the sky
the white-eyed vireo's call
the sweet curry's burn
whenever you touch my arm

the way a silence large as the Dust Bowl
deserves a name
so even those who were not there
can talk about it
the way weathermen talk about Katrina or Hazel
cartographers speak of The Great Divide

The first time mom had to search for my name
I looked her in the eyes with so much more
than our trip to the Outer Banks
than dogwood along the Blue Ridge
than black-eyed peas on a bed of steaming greens
and we named the silence Dixon
after the park where she pushed me on the swings
where we laughed and chased the squirrels.

One day, either too soon or not,
I will walk alone into that forest
and forget the way back;
I will climb the most ancient sycamore
whose name must surely be forgotten
and forget the way down.
As the sun begins to set
I will forget how to dream and that I cannot fly.

Unfettered

The Fool does not see
the hidden Hermit
behind his bright beacon,
only feels
the lightness of his valise
and the unfolding day
arcing like a rainbow.
If he thought about it,
the Fool would know
he cannot return
and sundown will
leave him exhausted
with a case to unpack—
silks and dragonflies,
poetry and krugerrands.
For dinner a bowl of rice
and a handful of sweet
sweet cherries.
The Fool
never has to sleep alone
but often chooses so
and come morning
when he cannot find
his sundries
sets off
again to follow
the twisted trail
leading
toward that inevitable glow

and fifty years
spinning by
before he arrives
in the desert
to relieve the Hermit
of his burdensome light.

One Possible Answer

Neither frightened nor amused
walking through the wild forest
trail winding its inevitable way toward the black water
I do not know how many furlongs or unseen deer will spy
      my passage
how many meadows—poppy and paintbrush and clover
how many clear streams
sunfish swimming beneath tiny waterfalls.

I will see sparrow and jay and ubiquitous mockingbird
squirrel and maybe a bobcat
a coyote or two—
perhaps a heron will unfold prayerful wings and rise
      from the swamp
a hunting kestrel will hover then dive.

What better thing than to wander and be astonished?

Having walked my allotted miles and reached the dark
      river
I will not look at these hands and ask
what have you accomplished or where have you been
or even were you grateful.
Neither amused nor frightened
I will reach into worn pockets
and find I have saved exactly two pennies—
that the boatman's open palm is warm and welcoming.

Outside Bozeman on a Winter's Solstice

Tonight, out here on the high plains
Zephyr romances the moon.
I watch this afternoon's snow
lifted and dancing in swirling currents,
as Diana shines
flirting, a princess at the ball.

But both know her course
was set long before the carving of these plateaus
and come morning Diana must return to the hunt.
They will encounter one another
as many more times as past, but no other night
will be near so cold, so clear, so perfect.
And this anguished certainty compels
Zephyr to scrawl his ephemeral words
infinitely fine.

Come tomorrow I will ride into town
and mail this letter. I trust it finds you
prosperous and well.